More Messy People

PEOPLE

Leader Guide

Praise for More Messy People

Jennifer has mastered the craft of creating fearless and transformative resources. Whether used for individual, small group or all-church study, *More Messy People* serves as a powerful reminder of what God can do in the lives of people just like us!

—**Shane L. Bishop**, Senior Pastor, Christ Church, Fairview Heights, Illinois, author of *That's Good News* and the *The Ping Life*

Well into my sixth decade of life, I have learned a truth that Jennifer so beautifully illustrates in *More Messy People*. It's this simple, yet profound truth. "Don't put a period where God puts a comma." Failure is common to our human existence. Whether they result from our family dysfunction or just making bad choices, God has an amazing and supernatural capacity to transform tragedy into triumph. Jen creatively helps us connect the lives of disordered women and men in the Bible to our lives and together discover the God who loves us most and best.

—**Rev. Dr. Jorge Acevedo**, leadership coach, writer, speaker, retired pastor

Available Component:

More Messy People

9781791033460 Print
9781791033477 ePub

More Messy People: Leader Guide

9781791033484 Print
9781791033491 ePub

More Messy People: DVD

9781791033507

Streaming video for *More Messy People* is available at AmplifyMedia.com.

Also Available from Jennifer Cowart

Messy People
Fierce
Pursued
Thrive

More Messy PEOPLE

LIFE LESSONS *from* IMPERFECT BIBLICAL HEROES

a Bible Study by

JENNIFER COWART

Abingdon Women | Nashville

More Messy People
Life Lessons from Imperfect Biblical Heroes
Leader Guide

ISBN 978-1-7910-3348-4

MANUFACTURED IN THE UNITED STATES OF AMERICA

Contents

About the Leader Guide Writer

Sally Sharpe is a spiritual director who is passionate about companioning others on the spiritual journey and helping them to experience the transformative love of God, which leads to healing and living fully as one's authentic self. With certificates in Spiritual Direction and Ignatian Spirituality from the Selah School of Spiritual Formation, she offers spiritual direction to individuals and groups, leads contemplative soul care retreats, and accompanies others through the Spiritual Exercises of Saint Ignatius (see www.sallysharpe.net). Formerly, she was Senior Editor of Abingdon Women, a series of in-depth Bible studies she developed and helped to launch and grow into a thriving line.

About the Author

Jennifer Cowart is the executive and teaching pastor at Harvest Church in Warner Robins, Georgia, which she and her husband, Jim, began in 2001. With degrees in Christian education, counseling, and business, Jen oversees a wide variety of ministries and enjoys doing life and ministry with others. As a gifted Bible teacher, Jen brings biblical truth to life through humor, authenticity, and everyday application. She is the author of four women's Bible studies (*Thrive*, *Pursued*, *Fierce*, and *Messy People*) and several small group studies coauthored with her husband, Jim, including *The One*, *Grounded in Prayer*, and *Living the Five*. They love doing life with their kids, Alyssa, Josh, Andrew, Hannah, and the newest addition, their grandson, Jordi.

Follow Jen:

 jimandjennifercowart

 jimandjennifer.cowart

Website: jennifercowart.org or jimandjennifercowart.org
        (check here for event dates and booking information)

Join Jen Cowart
for a one-of-a-kind study experience!

As Bible teacher and life-long learner, Jen loves to connect with other women studying the Bible and exploring faith. She offers a virtual drop in visit for groups studying *More Messy People* or her other women's Bible studies.

Whether you're just starting the first session and would love some inspiration straight from the author or you've spent several weeks together in this experience, Jen invites you to contact her directly through email at **Jennifer@harvestchurch4u.org** to see what can be arranged!

Join Jen as she explores how God used imperfect biblical heroes and and how God can use each of us and our own messy lives in powerful ways..

Introduction

Welcome to *More Messy People*, a six-week study of imperfect biblical heroes. A few years ago I began to ponder the amazing reality that God's heroes had messy stories. They led lives that ebbed and flowed with faithfulness and fruitfulness. That is relatable to me because my life also is rarely neat and tidy. My life is a messy one, and I'm guessing yours is too, at times.

As I continued pondering messy lives, I wrote a Bible study, *Messy People*. In it I examined six flawed but powerful people of Scripture and how they allowed God to turn their messes into His masterpieces. Because the idea of allowing God to do something positive with our messes resonated with many people, and there's no shortage of messy people in the Bible or in life, I decided to write another study, *More Messy People*.

In this study we will dig into the lives of six more biblical heroes—ordinary people who led extraordinary lives because they turned their messes over to God and found that their faithfulness in the hands of the Almighty could bring some magnificent results! Together we will explore the lives of two sisters, Rachel and Leah, along with Moses and Elijah from the Old Testament. Then we will move into the New Testament and explore another set of sisters, Martha and Mary, along with the great leaders Peter and Paul. Each of their stories will help us see that God chooses to use imperfect people to do incredible things when we turn to Him with our doubts and troubles.

About the Participant Workbook

Before the first session, you will want to distribute copies of the participant workbook to the members of your group. Be sure to communicate that they are to complete the first week of readings before your first group session. For each week there are five devotional lessons that combine study of Scripture with personal reflection and application. On average, each lesson can be completed in about twenty to thirty minutes. Completing these readings each week will prepare the women for the discussion and activities of the group session.

About This Leader Guide

As you gather each week with the members of your group, you will have the opportunity to watch a video, discuss and respond to what you're learning, and pray together. You will need access to a television and a DVD player with working remotes. Or, if you prefer, you may purchase streaming video files at www.Cokesbury.com, or you may access the videos for this study and other Abingdon Women Bible studies on AmplifyMedia.com with a membership subscription.

This leader guide and the video lessons will be your primary tools for leading each group session. In this book you will find outlines for six group sessions, each formatted for either a 60-minute or 90-minute group session:

60-Minute Format

Leader Prep (Before the Session)

Welcome and Opening Prayer	5 minutes
Icebreaker	5 minutes
Video	20 minutes
Group Discussion	25 minutes
Closing Prayer	5 minutes

90-Minute Format

Leader Prep (Before the Session)

Welcome and Opening Prayer	5-10 minutes
Icebreaker	5 minutes
Video	20 minutes

Group Discussion	25-35 minutes
Deeper Conversation	15 minutes
Closing Prayer	5 minutes

As you can see, the 90-minute format is identical to the 60-minute format but allows more time for the welcome/opening prayer and group discussion plus a Deeper Conversation exercise for small groups. Feel free to adapt or modify either of these formats, as well as the individual segments and activities, in any way to meet the specific needs and preferences of your group.

Here is a brief overview of the elements included in both formats:

Leader Prep (Before the Session)

For your preparation prior to the group session, this section provides an Overview of the week's biblical theme, and a list of materials and equipment needed. Be sure to review this section, as well as read through the *entire* session outline, before your group time in order to plan and prepare. If you choose, you also may find it helpful to watch the video lesson in advance.

Welcome and Opening Prayer (5-10 minutes, depending on session length)

Create a warm, welcoming environment as the women are gathering before the session begins. Consider either lighting one or more candles, providing coffee or other refreshments, or playing worship music, or all of these. (Bring a smartphone or tablet and a portable speaker if desired.) Be sure to provide nametags if the women do not know one another or you have new participants in your group. Then, when you are ready to begin, open the group in prayer before you begin your time.

You also may find it helpful to read aloud the week's Overview found in the Leader Prep section if not all group members have completed their homework.

Icebreaker (5 minutes)

Use the Icebreaker to briefly engage the women in the topic while helping them feel comfortable with one another.

Video (20 minutes)

Next, watch the week's video segment together. Be sure to direct participants to the Video Viewer Guide in the participant workbook, which they may complete as they watch the video. (Answers are provided on page 59 of this guide and page 204 in the participant workbook.)

Group Discussion (25-35 minutes, depending on session length)

After watching the video, choose from the questions provided to facilitate group discussion (questions are provided for both the video segment and the participant workbook material). For the participant workbook portion, you may choose to read aloud the discussion points or express them in your own words; then use one or more of the questions that follow to guide your conversation.

Note that more material is provided than you will have time to include. Before the session, select what questions you want to ask, putting a check mark beside them in your book. Reflect on each question and make some notes in the margins to share during your discussion time. Page references are provided for those questions that relate to specific questions or activities in the participant workbook. For these questions, invite group members to turn in their books to the pages indicated. Participants will need Bibles in order to look up various supplementary Scriptures.

Depending on the number of women in your group and the level of their participation, you may not have time to cover everything you have selected, and that is okay. Rather than attempting to bulldoze through, follow the Spirit's lead and be open to where the Spirit takes the conversation. Remember that your role is not to have all the answers but to encourage discussion and sharing.

Deeper Conversation (15 minutes)

If your group is meeting for 90 minutes, use this exercise for deeper sharing in small groups, dividing into groups of two or three. This is a time for women to share more intimately and build connections with one another. (Encourage the women to break into different groups each week.) Give a two-minute warning before time is up so that the groups may wrap up their discussion.

Closing Prayer (5 minutes)

Close by leading the group in prayer. If you'd like, invite the women to briefly name prayer requests. To get things started, you might share a personal request of your own. As women share their requests, model for the group by writing each request in your participant workbook, indicating that you will remember to pray for them during the week.

As the study progresses, you might encourage members to participate in the Closing Prayer by praying out loud for one another and the requests given. Ask the women to volunteer to pray for specific requests, or have each woman pray for the woman on her right or left. Make sure nametags are visible so that group members do not feel awkward if they do not remember someone's name.

Before You Begin

Life is filled with messy moments. Sometimes those messy moments become messy seasons. My hope is that this study will offer encouragement, hope, and some tools for moving forward.

Friend, you have the incredible opportunity to lead others in this journey as you explore how God loves working in the lives of messy people—because messy people are all He has to work with! Your role is not to have all the answers but simply to offer acceptance, compassion, and encouragement along the way. Take a moment now to thank God for this privilege and to ask for guidance, wisdom, and patience for the journey.

May you and the women in your group get so close to Jesus that you freely and fearlessly put your hand in his and invite him to turn your messes into his masterpieces! I'm praying for you and cheering you on.

From one messy person to another, let's do this!

Jen

Leader Helps

Preparing for the Sessions

- Decide whether you will use the 60-minute or 90-minute format. Be sure to communicate dates and times to participants in advance.
- Ensure that participants receive their workbooks at least one week before your first session and instruct them to complete the first week's devotional lessons. If you have the phone numbers or email addresses of your group members, send out a reminder and a welcome.
- Check out your meeting space before each group session (or set up a virtual meeting and share the link). Make sure the room is ready. Do you have enough chairs? Do you have the equipment and supplies you need? (See the list of materials needed in each session outline.)
- Pray for your group and each group member by name. Ask God to work in the life of every woman in your group.
- Read and complete the week's devotional lessons in the participant workbook and review the session outline in the leader guide. Select the discussion points and questions you want to cover and make some notes in the margins to share in your discussion time.

Leading the Sessions

- Personally welcome and greet each woman as she arrives (whether in person or online). You might want to have a sign-up list for the women to record their names and contact information.

- At the start of each session, ask the women to turn off or silence their cell phones (or eliminate other distractions if meeting online).

- Always start on time. Honor the time of those who are punctual.

- Encourage everyone to participate fully, but don't put anyone on the spot. Be prepared to offer a personal example or answer if no one else responds at first.

- Communicate the importance of completing the weekly devotional lessons and participating in group discussion.

- Facilitate but don't dominate. Remember that if you talk most of the time, group members may tend to listen rather than to engage. Your task is to encourage conversation and keep the discussion moving.

- If someone monopolizes the conversation, kindly thank her for sharing and ask if anyone else has any insights.

- Try not to interrupt, judge, or minimize anyone's comments or input.

- Remember that you are not expected to be the expert or have all the answers. Acknowledge that all of you are on this journey together, with the Holy Spirit as your leader and guide. If issues or questions arise that you don't feel equipped to handle or answer, talk with the pastor or a staff member at your church.

- Don't rush to fill the silence. If no one speaks right away, it's okay to wait for someone to answer. After a moment, ask, "Would anyone be willing to share?" If no one responds, try asking the question again a different way—or offer a brief response and ask if anyone has anything to add.

- Encourage good discussion, but don't be timid about calling time on a particular question and moving ahead. Part of your responsibility is to keep the group on track. If you decide to spend extra time on a given question or activity, consider skipping or spending less time on another question or activity in order to stay on schedule.

- End on time. If you are running over, give members the opportunity to leave if they need to. Then wrap up as quickly as you can.
- Thank the women for coming and let them know you're looking forward to seeing them next time.
- Be prepared for some women to want to hang out and talk at the end. If you need everyone to leave by a certain time, communicate this at the beginning of the group session. If you are meeting in a church during regularly scheduled activities, be aware of nursery closing times.

WEEK 1

Leah and Rachel

Overcoming Jealousy

Genesis 25–31; 35; 37

Leader Prep (Before the Session)

Overview

This week we looked at the lives of two sisters, Leah and Rachel, who were thrust into a love triangle when they wound up married to the same man. Jacob had worked for seven years to marry the woman he loved, Rachel. But in an ironic twist of fate, Jacob—whose name means deceiver—was tricked by his uncle Laban into marrying Rachel's older sister, Leah. He then took Rachel as his wife too, agreeing to work another seven years for Laban. What followed this bridal altar switch was a baby-making competition between the two sisters, resulting in jealousy, rivalry, deceit, and even hatred. The dysfunction not only affected them but also passed from one generation to the next. Yet from this messy lineage came kings, prophets, warriors, heroes, and even the Messiah Himself. God created a masterpiece from their mess!

If God can choose, bless, and use a family with as much baggage as the family these two sisters became a part of, then we can have hope. God chooses and uses messy people like us. All we have to do is choose to let God redeem our messiness.

Main Takeaway

We overcome jealousy when we realize that God wants us, as we are, in His family. In God's eyes, we are loved, chosen, and more than enough!

Memory Verse

God decided in advance to adopt us into his own family by bringing us to himself through Jesus Christ. This is what he wanted to do, and it gave him great pleasure.

(*Ephesians* 1:5 NLT)

What You Will Need

- *More Messy People* DVD and DVD player, or equipment to stream the video online
- Bible and *More Messy People* participant workbook for reference
- Markerboard or chart paper and markers (optional)
- Stick-on nametags and markers (optional)
- Smartphone or tablet and portable speaker (optional)

Session Outline

Welcome and Opening Prayer (5-10 minutes, depending on session length)

In order to create a warm, welcoming environment as the women are gathering before the session begins, consider either lighting one or more candles, providing coffee or other refreshments, or playing worship music, or all of these. (Bring a smartphone or tablet and a portable speaker if desired.) Be sure to provide nametags if the women do not know one another or you have new participants in your group. Then, when you are ready to begin, open the group in prayer.

If meeting online, welcome each participant as she joins and encourage the women to talk informally until you are ready to open the group in prayer.

Icebreaker (5 minutes)

Invite the women to share short responses to the following question:

- What's the biggest, literal mess you've ever been responsible for, and what kind of help did you need to clean it up?

Video (20 minutes)

Play the Week 1 video segment. Invite participants to complete the Video Viewer Guide for Week 1 in the participant workbook as they watch (page 42).

Group Discussion (25-35 minutes, depending on session length)

Note: More material is provided than you will have time to include. Before the session, select what you want to cover.

- What are the two simple, but not necessarily easy, steps that can help us to defeat the green-eyed monster of jealousy?
- Read aloud Philippians 4:11-13. How does gratitude help us to live out these verses?
- Why do we often find it easier to comfort those who are hurting than to celebrate those who are rejoicing? What are some practical ways we can rejoice with others?

Participant Workbook Discussion Questions

1. In Day 1 of our study we stepped into the messy lives of Jacob, Leah, and Rachel and the idea that sometimes our dreams in life are disrupted. We also were introduced to the overarching theme of this study—that God can take whatever messes we're dealing with and bring something amazing from them when we trust in Him.
   - How was Jacob's life an ironic twist of events?
   - How do you imagine that Jacob, the deceiver, felt when he realized he had been deceived at the altar and had married Leah instead of his beloved Rachel?
   - What dreams did you have as a child? Which of those dreams are you now living out? Which of those dreams have become complicated or filled with pain? (page 17)
   - Have someone read aloud Ephesians 2:10. How does this verse challenge and/or encourage you?

2. During Day 2 of our study, we saw that Leah and Rachel were part of a long line of family dysfunction. Their mother-in-law, Rebekah, their father, Laban, and their shared husband, Jacob, were all deceivers. Jacob conned his brother out of his birthright, Rebekah helped Jacob deceive Isaac out of his blessing, and Laban tricked his son-in-law with a bridal altar switch that resulted in a double union. The result of this deceitful double union was conflict, competition, and contempt that not only affected them but also impacted their children, continuing the dysfunction for generations. Yet God blessed this messy family bloodline.
   - Read aloud Genesis 29:22-30 or retell the story in your own words. What might have been happening behind the scenes when Laban tricked Jacob into marrying Leah instead of Rachel? What do you imagine all

of those involved might have been thinking and feeling (Laban, Laban's wife, Jacob, Leah, and Rachel)?

- What do we observe from this family about the nature or pattern of family dysfunction? (page 22)
- How has family dysfunction affected *you*? How can you move beyond the mess and dysfunction to a healthy way of living? (page 24)
- On a scale of 1–10, with 1 being very easy and 10 being very difficult, how easy or difficult it is for you to believe that God loves you even in your messiness. Explain your answer. (page 21)
- Have someone read aloud 1 Peter 2:9. What does it mean to you personally to know you are chosen by God?

3. On Day 3 we focused on Leah and her journey from trying to win her husband's approval to praising God. Leah couldn't change the circumstances she found herself in. She couldn't change the hearts of her family. But she came to realize that she could change herself. She could praise God for what she had. And we can do the same.
    - Read aloud Genesis 29:16-18. What do we learn about Laban's daughters in these verses? What do most scholars believe the phrase "weak eyes" implies about Leah?
    - As a child, were you ever compared to someone else unfavorably? How has this comparison affected you? (page 27)
    - What does Genesis 29:31a tell us that would have added to Leah's pain? (page 27) How did God respond?
    - How do Leah's remarks at the birth of her first three sons show us that she hoped to gain the approval of her husband? (Refer to Genesis 29:31-35 and the list you wrote on page 28.) What subtle but powerful shift do we see upon the birth of her fourth son?
    - Praising God for what we have helps to keep us from getting stuck in our pain for what we don't have. Share some of the praises you recorded on page 29.

4. On Day 4 we saw that Rachel and Leah were plagued with the same demon: jealousy. Leah was jealous of the love Jacob had for Rachel. Rachel was jealous of Leah's fertility. They both fell victim to the comparison trap.

Comparison steals joy and leaves us wanting more. It leads to discontent with our current situation and makes peace seem elusive.

- How do we see the rivalry between the sisters play out in Genesis 30:1-24? What does each sister do? (page 32) How do we see jealousy at work in this rivalry?
- In what areas of your life do you find yourself playing the comparison game—perhaps wanting what someone else has? How have comparison and jealousy affected you in the past—physically, mentally, emotionally, and spiritually? (page 33)
- What might Rachel's actions in Genesis 31:34-35 reveal about her trust in God?
- Read aloud Philippians 4:11-13. What is Paul's meaning in these verses? (page 33)
- How can you be content today? Where can you find joy? (page 36)

5. During our Day 5 lesson we saw that despite the messiness and dysfunction of Jacob's family, God loved them and did not stop pursuing them. God not only blessed both Rachel and Leah with sons, God also blessed Jacob, fulfilling a promise He had given to Jacob's grandfather, Abraham. Jesus himself is a descendant of Jacob's family. God chooses and uses messy people, and God wants us in His family.
   - Read aloud Genesis 35:9-12. How did God bless Jacob? How did this fulfill a promise God had given to his grandfather, Abraham, in Genesis 12:1-3? (page 38)
   - How does it encourage you to know that Jesus came from the lineage of Jacob's messy family? What does this say about God?
   - What generational cycles do you want God to break through you? What next step is God inviting you to take on the journey from messy to masterpiece? (page 40)
   - Read aloud Ephesians 1:5 and Romans 10:9. How do these verses speak to God's desire for us to be part of His family? What is God's part, and what is our part?
   - How has your study this week helped to build your trust in God?

Deeper Conversation (15 minutes)

Divide into smaller groups of 2 to 3 for deeper conversation about practical application using three "So, what...?" questions. (Encourage the women to break into different groups each week.) If you'd like, before the session, write the questions on a markerboard or chart paper.

- So, *what* did you learn/discover this week—about God, yourself, or others?
- So, *what* is God inviting or calling you to do in response?
- So, *what* encouragement have you received for moving forward?

Closing Prayer (5 minutes)

Close the session by taking personal prayer requests from group members and leading the group in prayer. As you progress to later weeks in the study, you might encourage members to participate by praying out loud for one another and the requests given.

WEEK 2

Moses

Learning to Trust God

Exodus 1–17;
Numbers 11; 20

Leader Prep (Before the Session)

Overview

This week we focused on the messy life of Moses, who:

- was born a Hebrew slave,
- was raised in Pharaoh's palace,
- committed murder,
- escaped to Midian as a fugitive,
- encountered God in a burning bush,
- warned Pharaoh of ten plagues (which then were carried out), and
- led his people out of Egypt and through the wilderness.

There were signs and wonders all along the way, including the Red Sea parting for the people to walk across on dry ground, manna appearing on the ground in the mornings to feed them, and water gushing from a rock—twice—to quench their thirst. However, the second time God brought water from a rock, Moses did not obey God's instructions, so Moses was not allowed to enter the Promised Land. Despite all the messes along his journey, Moses's life was a masterpiece of truly biblical proportions. As Deuteronomy 34:10 (NLT) tells us, "There has never been another prophet in Israel like Moses, whom the LORD knew face to face."

We can learn from Moses's example to become faithful disciples who persevere despite challenges and setbacks, trusting God at all times.

Main Takeaway

There will be hard seasons; but if we don't give up, we can push through with God, trusting Him to be faithful.

Memory Verse

So do not fear, for I am with you;
    do not be dismayed, for I am your God.
I will strengthen you and help you;
    I will uphold you with my righteous right hand.
                    (Isaiah 41:10)

What You Will Need

- *More Messy People* DVD and DVD player, or equipment to stream the video online
- Bible and *More Messy People* participant workbook for reference
- Markerboard or chart paper and markers (optional)
- Stick-on nametags and markers (optional)
- Smartphone or tablet and portable speaker (optional)

Session Outline

Welcome and Opening Prayer (5-10 minutes, depending on session length)

In order to create a warm, welcoming environment as the women are gathering before the session begins, consider either lighting one or more candles, providing coffee or other refreshments, or playing worship music, or all of these. (Bring a smartphone or tablet and a portable speaker if desired.) Be sure to provide nametags if the women do not know one another or you have new participants in your group. Then, when you are ready to begin, open the group in prayer.

If meeting online, welcome each participant as she joins and encourage the women to talk informally until you are ready to open the group in prayer.

Icebreaker (5 minutes)

Invite the women to share short responses to the following question:

- When have you been discouraged and wanted to give up?

Video (20 minutes)

Play the Week 2 video segment. Invite participants to complete the Video Viewer Guide for Week 2 in the participant workbook as they watch (pages 74-75).

Group Discussion (25-35 minutes, depending on session length)

Note: More material is provided than you will have time to include. Before the session, select what you want to cover.

Video Discussion Questions

- When we feel we're not good enough, what do we need to remember about God? When has your inadequacy increased your dependence on God?
- Why is it important to obey immediately even when we don't understand completely? Who are some of the people in Scripture who model this for us?
- How can it encourage us to remember that everyone has critics in life?
- How can 2 Corinthians 12:9 encourage us when we feel unqualified?
- Has there ever been a time when you knew God was calling you but you hoped someone else would step forward? What happened?

Participant Workbook Discussion Questions

1. On Day 1 we learned about Moses's life from his miraculous rescue as an infant to his flight to Midian after killing an Egyptian. From start to finish, Moses's life was messy, but he also learned to walk incredibly close to God. His faith and maturity were not automatic. He had to learn to deal with his emotions and limitations and move through them. But what a powerful example he is of someone who struggled and prevailed through faith.
   - What stands out to you from the biblical account of Moses's early life found in Exodus 2:1-10? Though we don't have the details of how Moses grew up, how do you imagine being raised by Pharaoh's daughter might have influenced him?
   - Read Exodus 2:11-12 aloud. How do these verses support the idea that Moses knew of his Hebrew heritage? How do they help to explain—not justify—Moses's actions? (page 48)
   - According to Exodus 2:13-15, how did Moses discover that what he had done was no longer a secret? What happened next? (page 49)

- Like Moses, our emotions sometimes spill over, causing us to make a mess of things. How can we try to make things right when this happens? What can help us to deal with our messes in ways that honor God?

2. On Day 2 we explored Moses's encounter with God at the burning bush. In this epic meeting, God revealed His name, His promise, and His mission for Moses. We also examined three of the five excuses that Moses offered God. Though we may be guilty of all three excuses at times, often there is a particular excuse that we tend to give on a regular basis. Moses eventually moved past his excuses as his trust and confidence in God grew, and the same can be true for us.
    - What stood out to you about Moses's dynamic encounter with God at the burning bush, found in Exodus 3 and 4? What did God reveal is His name (3:14), His promise (3:12), and His mission for Moses (3:10)?
    - What were the three excuses of Moses that we considered on Day 2? What was Moses's concern or fear related to each excuse? Which of these three excuses resonates most with you, and why?
    - Sometimes we view excuses as humility, but what do they really reveal? What are some of the questions that have served as excuses for you? (page 52)
    - Recall a time when feeling inadequate, wanting a plan, or fearing criticism kept you from saying yes to God. What were you believing—or not believing—about yourself or about God?
    - How might God be calling you to partner with Him and move out of the shallows into unknown waters now? (pages 53 and 55)
    - How can remembering God's faithfulness to us in the past help us when we're tempted to make excuses? What are some moments from your past when God was faithful to you? (Refer to your list on page 57.)

3. On Day 3 we looked at two more excuses Moses offered God at the burning bush—excuses we all can relate to. Identifying our excuses and then asking God to help us move beyond them in faith is what moves us from messy to masterpiece. Following Jesus means we let go of our excuses and our selfish desires and trust God with our lives, being ready to move into action at His invitation.

- Read aloud Luke 9:23. How would you explain what it means to take up your cross and follow Jesus? What does this require?
- Read Exodus 4:10-12. What was Moses's excuse and God's response? When have you felt unqualified for the task God was calling you to do? (page 60)
- Read Exodus 4:14-17. What was the bottom-line excuse within Moses's plea for God to send someone else? How would you summarize God's response? (page 61)
- Is there something you are reluctant to do now that you know God wants you to do? How does knowing that God is already at work providing for your needs encourage you? (pages 61-62)

4. During our Day 4 lesson we took a big picture view of Moses's journey, pausing at a moment when Moses was feeling discouraged and worn down by the people's complaining. We know what it feels like when discouragement sets in and we want to give up. In those moments, we need to do what Moses did: cry out to the Lord!
   - What are some of your negative "what ifs"? How could you rewrite those what if's as positive what-if possibilities? (page 65)
   - Read aloud Numbers 11:10-15. What might you have said to God if you were in Moses's shoes? (page 66) When has discouragement set in and made you want to give up on what God has called you to do? (page 67)
   - What does God promise in 1 Thessalonians 5:24? In addition to being with us, what three things does God promise in Isaiah 41:10 to do for us? (page 67)
   - What are some practical ways we can cry out to God and claim God's promises in times of discouragement?
   - Read aloud Philippians 1:6. Is there a circumstance or area of your life in which you need to apply this verse?

5. During our lesson for Day 5 we focused on a time when Moses was disobedient. Instead of obeying God's instructions, Moses did what he had successfully done in a prior similar situation. In most instances, that would make sense, but in this case, God had given new instructions. Because all disobedience has consequences, Moses had to experience the

consequences of his choice to do things his own way. But this did not mean God stopped loving Moses; in fact, we know that Moses had a very close relationship with God. And Scripture tells us that his life was a masterpiece of truly biblical proportions.

- What did God instruct Moses to do in Exodus 17:6? What is different about God's instructions to Moses in Numbers 20:7-12? (page 71) Why do you think this is a problem of significance? (page 72)
- According to Numbers 20:12, what was the consequence for Moses's disobedience? (page 73)
- When have *you* heard God speak to you but then proceeded to do things your own way? What was the outcome? (page 72)
- Based on Deuteronomy 34:10, how can we know that Moses's disobedience did not negate all the good he had done or weaken his relationship with God?
- How does Moses's life encourage or inspire you?

Deeper Conversation (15 minutes)

Divide into smaller groups of 2 to 3 for deeper conversation about practical application using some "So, what...?" questions. (Encourage the women to break into different groups each week.) If you'd like, before the session, write the questions on a markerboard or chart paper.

- So, *what* did you learn/discover this week—about God, yourself, or others?
- So, *what* is God inviting or calling you to do in response?
- So, *what* encouragement have you received for moving forward?

Closing Prayer (5 minutes)

Close the session by taking personal prayer requests from group members and leading the group in prayer. As you progress to later weeks in the study, you might encourage members to participate by praying out loud for one another and the requests given.

WEEK 3

Elijah

Balancing Faith and Emotion

1 Kings 16–19

Leader Prep (Before the Session)

Overview

This week we considered the life of Elijah, a prophet of the Old Testament. In a culture defined by wickedness and idolatry, he stood as a man of courage, holiness, and uncompromising faith. Elijah confronted the wicked King Ahab, boldly prophesying there would be no rain in Israel for over three years, and it happened just as he said. God got the people's attention through the resulting famine, yet this made Elijah extremely unpopular with the king and his equally wicked wife, Jezebel. Elijah fled to safety, where God miraculously cared for him. When he returned three years later, Elijah confronted King Ahab once again and had a great showdown with 450 prophets of Baal on Mount Carmel, which demonstrated God's power and brought the people back to God. Despite this high moment and the return of rain to the land, Elijah had a death sentence on his head; and he struggled with depression and even suicidal thoughts.

Elijah was a messy person. Yet, through faith, courage, and his dependence on the Lord, he persevered and learned to balance his faith and emotions; and he is hailed as one of the greatest figures in all of Scripture.

Main Takeaway

With courageous perseverance, people to support us, and prayer, we can remain faithful even through the most difficult and darkest seasons of life.

Memory Verse

"Have I not commanded you? Be strong and courageous. Do not be afraid; do not be discouraged, for the Lord your God will be with you wherever you go."

(Joshua 1:9)

What You Will Need

- *More Messy People* DVD and DVD player, or equipment to stream the video online
- Bible and *More Messy People* participant workbook for reference
- Markerboard or chart paper and markers (optional)
- Stick-on nametags and markers (optional)
- Smartphone or tablet and portable speaker (optional)

Session Outline

Welcome and Opening Prayer (5-10 minutes, depending on session length)

In order to create a warm, welcoming environment as the women are gathering before the session begins, consider either lighting one or more candles, providing coffee or other refreshments, or playing worship music, or all of these. (Bring a smartphone or tablet and a portable speaker if desired.) Be sure to provide nametags if the women do not know one another or you have new participants in your group. Then, when you are ready to begin, open the group in prayer.

If meeting online, welcome each participant as she joins and encourage the women to talk informally until you are ready to open the group in prayer.

Icebreaker (5 minutes)

Invite the women to share a short response to the following question:

- What is one way God has provided or cared for you recently?

Video (20 minutes)

Play the Week 3 video segment. Invite participants to complete the Video Viewer Guide for Week 3 in the participant workbook as they watch (page 105).

Group Discussion (25-35 minutes, depending on session length)

Note: More material is provided than you will have time to include. Before the session, select what you want to cover.

<u>Video Discussion Questions</u>

- What helps you to stand for God's truth even when it's hard?
- In what area of your life do you need to trust God right now?
- How well do you rest?
- How have you experienced the power of prayer?
- Who left you a legacy of faith? Who is counting on you to leave them a legacy of faith?

<u>Participant Workbook Discussion Questions</u>

1. Day 1 gave us an overview of Elijah's life, laying the foundation for our study this week. Elijah's life was a roller coaster. He experienced incredible highs and debilitating lows. He performed miracles and stood for God in powerful ways in a culture consumed with wickedness. Elijah experienced firsthand God's care in the details of his life. But he also struggled with depression and even suicidal thoughts. Like the other biblical heroes we have studied, Elijah was a messy person, and his story has many timeless truths to teach us.
   - What are we told about Elijah in 1 Kings 17:1? What did Elijah prophesy? (page 79)
   - How would you summarize God's purpose for raising up the prophet Elijah against King Ahab and Queen Jezebel?
   - When has a difficult situation forced you to focus more completely on God and His standards? What was the outcome? (page 80)
   - What initial thoughts do you have after reading Elijah's story in 1 Kings 17–19 and 2 Kings 1–2? (Refer to your notes on page 81.)

2. On Day 2 we learned the unusual ways God provided and cared for Elijah while he was in hiding from the king and queen. God's ways are often beyond our understanding, yet even when we don't know what God is up to, we can be confident that He is working on our behalf.

- Read aloud Matthew 10:30. How does this verse encourage you that God cares about the details of your life? Share your response to God's care for you that you wrote on page 83.
- In what unusual ways did God provide for Elijah's needs according to 1 Kings 17:2-16? (page 84)
- How do you think the widow of Zarephath's faith was impacted by what God did after Elijah's arrival? (page 84)
- Read aloud Isaiah 55:8-9. What important insight regarding the way God works do we find in these verses? (page 85)
- When has God called *you* to do something scary when you didn't understand all that God was doing? How did you respond? (page 85)

3. On Day 3 we saw that God called Elijah to confront King Ahab once again, and what followed was the great showdown between Elijah and 450 prophets of Baal on Mount Carmel. In the face of evil, Elijah did not shirk away from doing what was right but approached the task God had set before him with a sense of authority and power. When God asks us to stand for truth, as Elijah did, we can ask God for the courage and strength to move forward despite our fears.
   - Read aloud 1 Kings 18:20-26 and 33-39. Then have fun sharing your own descriptions of what happened on Mount Carmel. (page 91)
   - When have you felt God prompting you to speak up for those who can't or won't speak up for themselves? How did you respond? (pages 89-90)
   - What issues do you see in our culture that Christians should be making a stand for today? Is there one that especially tugs at your heart? (page 90)
   - Where do you sense God calling *you* to be bold right now? Are any fears holding you back? (page 92) What do you need from God to move past your fear?

4. In our lesson on Day 4 we saw rain returning to the land after a three-year famine and Elijah running for his life when Jezebel imposed a death sentence on him. As Elijah fled to Beersheba, exhaustion caught up with him, and he reached a breaking point. After an angel tended to his needs, Elijah made his way to Mount Sinai where he wrestled with his feelings and heard from

the Lord in an unexpected way. When we struggle like Elijah, we, too, can be honest about how we're feeling and trust God to care for us and lead us in the way we should go.

- Review 1 Kings 18:40-46. What stands out to you in this account of what happened after the showdown at Mount Carmel, and why?
- What picture does 1 Kings 19:1-7 paint of Elijah's emotional and physical state? What is Elijah's plea in verse 4? How did God respond to Elijah's plea? (page 95)
- What are some unhealthy ways we can respond to difficult emotions, leading to undesirable outcomes? What are some healthy ways we can respond that leave us feeling better at the end of our struggle? (Refer to the ideas on page 96.)
- What can help us to determine where we are on the spectrum from exhaustion and discouragement to more serious depression requiring professional help? What are some sources of help where we can turn?
- According to 1 Kings 19:11-14, what did Elijah experience on the mountain, and how did he hear from God? How does this famous incident in Elijah's life speak to your own heart and life today?
- What can we learn from Elijah's story in 1 Kings 18 and 19 that can help us when we are facing times of confusion, doubt, discouragement, and even despair?

5. In our lesson for Day 5 we camped in 1 Kings 19:15-18, considering that when Elijah heard from God, he was given clarity about his purpose and his people. God knew Elijah was not done. He still had work to do, and he was not being asked to do it alone. Like Eiljah, we all need purpose and people, without whom we can easily slip into frustration, depression, and a distorted sense of reality.

- When has it been hard for you to hear God speak? What did it take for you to get to a place where you could clearly hear from God and His Word again? (page 102)
- According to 1 Kings 19:15-18, what was Elijah's purpose, and who were his people? (page 102)

- Do you have a spiritual tribe? If not, what steps can you take to build one?
- What purpose do you sense God calling you to in this season of life? (page 103) If you're unsure, how might God be working even now to give you clarity or guidance?
- Review the four lessons we've learned from Elijah this week, found on pages 80-81. Which one resonates with you most strongly now, and why?

Deeper Conversation (15 minutes)

Divide into smaller groups of 2 to 3 for deeper conversation about practical application using some "So, what...?" questions. (Encourage the women to break into different groups each week.) If you'd like, before the session, write the questions on a markerboard or chart paper.

- *So, what* did you learn/discover this week—about God, yourself, or others?
- *So, what* is God inviting or calling you to do in response?
- *So, what* encouragement have you received for moving forward?

Closing Prayer (5 minutes)

Close the session by taking personal prayer requests from group members and leading the group in prayer. As you progress to later weeks in the study, you might encourage members to participate by praying out loud for one another and the requests given.

WEEK 4

Mary and Martha

Establishing Priorities

Luke 9–10;
John 11–12

Leader Prep (Before the Session)

Overview

This week we focused on another set of sisters, Martha and Mary. Jesus knew what lay ahead for him in Jerusalem, and he needed a safe place to rest. He found that safe place in the small town of Bethany, just two miles east of Jerusalem, where Martha, Mary, and their brother, Lazarus, lived. Martha quickly extended an invitation of hospitality to Jesus and his disciples, but once her guests arrived, she became consumed by the tasks she felt needed to be done. Martha complained to Jesus that Mary was not helping her, and Jesus gently corrected her, commending Mary for her choice to sit at his feet—a choice that showed she had prioritized spending time with him above the demands of the world. We see Mary at the feet of Jesus once again after her brother's death, when she is burdened by grief (John 11), and at a special dinner given in Jesus's honor, when she is anointing his feet in an extravagant act of worship (John 12). Even so, in all three siblings we can find evidence suggesting a close relationship with Jesus as their friend and Savior; and as a result, they were available to be used by Jesus for his purposes. Despite their differences, they show us how to have an intimate relationship with Jesus built on love and trust.

Main Takeaway

When we prioritize time with Jesus, knowing Him as both friend and Savior, we can trust Him to be with us through the ups and downs of life, meeting all our needs.

Memory Verse

"But seek first his kingdom and his righteousness, and all these things will be given to you as well."

(Matthew 6:33)

What You Will Need

- *More Messy People* DVD and DVD player, or equipment to stream the video online
- Bible and *More Messy People* participant workbook for reference
- Markerboard or chart paper and markers (optional)
- Stick-on nametags and markers (optional)
- Smartphone or tablet and portable speaker (optional)

Session Outline

Welcome and Opening Prayer (5-10 minutes, depending on session length)

In order to create a warm, welcoming environment as the women are gathering before the session begins, consider lighting one or more candles, providing coffee or other refreshments, and/or playing worship music. (Bring a smartphone or tablet and a portable speaker if desired.) Be sure to provide nametags if the women do not know one another or you have new participants in your group. Then, when you are ready to begin, open the group in prayer.

If meeting online, welcome each participant as she joins and encourage the women to talk informally until you are ready to open the group in prayer.

Icebreaker (5 minutes)

Invite the women to share short responses to the following question:

- Do you tend to relate more to Martha or to Mary? There is no right or wrong answer here. Just share your first response without a lot of explanation.

Video (20 minutes)

Play the Week 4 video segment. Invite participants to complete the Video Viewer Guide for Week 4 in the participant workbook as they watch (page 136).

Group Discussion (25-35 minutes, depending on session length)

Note: More material is provided than you will have time to include. Before the session, select what you want to cover.

- When there are so many good things to be done, how do we prioritize in a way that is pleasing to the Lord?
- Of the seven tips for living out your priorities, which are more challenging for you, and why?

Participant Workbook Discussion Questions

1. In Day 1 we considered the growing hostility toward Jesus among the Pharisees, who began to plot against him. This greatly affected how he and his disciples were greeted as they traveled. So, Jesus and his disciples left the safety of the Galilee region and headed south, where they were warmly welcomed into the home of Martha, Mary, and Lazarus.
   - Read aloud Matthew 13:58. Based on what this verse tells us, what were the consequences for a town, family, or person who did not welcome Jesus in faith? (page 109)
   - In Luke 9:5, 58 and 10:5-12, what did Jesus tell his disciples to prepare them for an unwelcome response? (page 109)
   - According to Luke 10:38, what kind of reception did Jesus receive from Martha? (page 110)
   - Do you tend to be quick to offer your home or resources to others? If not, what holds you back? (page 110)
   - How can you help create a welcoming environment—in your home? in your church? in your Bible Study? (page 111)

2. On Day 2 we dug into the story of Martha and Mary as Jesus was a guest in their home. Many of us want to be like Mary, putting everything aside and just sitting at the feet of Jesus, but we're busy. So, we end up like Martha— well-intentioned but drowning in self-appointed, or maybe even other-appointed, tasks. It leaves us overwhelmed—and maybe even resentful. This scene shows us what matters most—choosing Jesus first.
   - Read aloud Luke 10:38-42. What had distracted Martha? When have you become so involved in serving that it negatively affected your relationship with God or others? (page 113)

- What did Martha say to Jesus? What do you hear in her choice of words? (page 114) When you feel overwhelmed like Martha, how does it affect you? How does it affect those around you? (page 115)
- How did Jesus respond to Martha, and how do you feel about his response?
- In verse 42, what words does Jesus use to describe Mary's choice? What does he mean by this?
- How do you handle the tension between wanting to sit at Jesus's feet and needing to get things done?

3. In our Day 3 lesson we acknowledged that we live in a world where a Martha-style work ethic is often expected. In fact, usually it's the person who is being productive, staying on top of things, and getting the work done who is admired and rewarded—or at the very least, appreciated. Yet Jesus told us, "Seek first his kingdom and his righteousness, and all these things will be given to you as well" (Matthew 6:33). This requires choosing our priorities intentionally.
   - Review Luke 10:38-42 once more. Based on this account, what would you list as Martha's priorities? (page 119)
   - How does the pace of your life affect your relationship with Jesus? (page 118) What keeps you distracted, worried, and upset? What keeps you from enjoying the presence of Christ daily? (page 121)
   - Read Matthew 6:33 aloud. Practically speaking, what does it mean to seek Jesus first in our lives? (page 120)
   - Have you ever been criticized, or criticized someone else, for prioritizing Jesus—for seeking God and His Kingdom first? If so, share about it briefly. (page 120)

4. On Day 4 we focused on Mary's devotion to Jesus. For some of us, finding peace and enjoying moments of stillness, like Mary, come naturally. For others, we relate more to Martha. We find a sense of worth in being productive. Yet our worth does not come from what we do but from who God is and who He says we are as members of His family. What Jesus most values is not our productivity but our devotion. And Mary understood this.

- Read aloud Luke 10:39, John 11:32, and John 12:3. Where is Mary positioned in each of these scenes? (See your answers on page 125.)

- How do we see others responding to Mary's choice to be at the feet of Jesus in Luke 10 and John 12? How does Jesus respond? (pages 125-126)

- If you were in Mary's place, sitting at the feet of Jesus, do you think you would be concerned about what others thought or said? Explain your response. (page 126)

- Who needs your whole face—your undivided attention—today, and how can you give it to them? How can you be more intentional in giving Jesus your whole face? (page 128)

5. On Day 5 we considered some additional takeaways we can glean from the story of Martha, Mary, and Lazarus. They enjoyed a close friendship with Jesus, they knew him as Lord and Savior, and they were available for his purposes. Yet the Bible doesn't paint them as perfect. It's good for us to see their humanity and remember that just as Jesus was with them through all their troubles, so he will be with us. He is faithful and true.

   - Read aloud John 11:5. What word describes Jesus's relationship with his friends? What clues do we find in Luke 10:38-42 that suggest their relationship was close? (page 131)

   - How does the story of Martha, Mary, and Lazarus suggest that personal relationship went beyond friendship to Lordship for all three? How can we make a case that each sibling believed in Jesus as Messiah?

   - How would you describe your relationship with Jesus? (page 134)

   - How was each sibling available for Jesus's purposes? What contributions in ministry did each one make? What purposes do you feel Jesus calling you to? How is He calling you to serve? (page 135)

   - If you could be an observer in one of the scenes we've explored this week in the lives of Martha, Mary, and Lazarus, which would you choose and why? (page 132)

Deeper Conversation (15 minutes)

Divide into smaller groups of 2 to 3 for deeper conversation about practical application using some "So, what...?" questions. (Encourage the women to break into different groups each week.) If you'd like, before the session, write the questions on a markerboard or chart paper.

- So, *what* did you learn/discover this week—about God, yourself, or others?
- So, *what* is God inviting or calling you to do in response?
- So, *what* encouragement have you received for moving forward?

Closing Prayer (5 minutes)

Close the session by taking personal prayer requests from group members and leading the group in prayer. Encourage members to participate by praying out loud for each other and the requests given.

WEEK 5

Peter

Growing Up into Christ

Matthew 14; 16; 18;
Luke 5; 22;
John 18; 21;
Acts 2; 10

Leader Prep (Before the Session)

Overview

This week we explored the life of a fisherman who became a fisher of men, Simon Peter. His life changed forever one morning on the shore of Lake Genneserat, also known as the Sea of Galilee, when a miraculous catch of fish led him to leave everything behind to follow Jesus.

Peter didn't always get it right. He doubted and began to sink when walking on the water to Jesus, he cut off the ear of a Roman soldier, and he denied Jesus three times. But we can't look at only these isolated moments. The bigger picture is the better glimpse into who he was—brave and faithful.

Peter's faith is inspirational. He trusted Jesus enough to do the scary thing and step out of the boat—the only disciple who risked walking on the water with Jesus. He boldly declared Jesus was the Messiah. And after having denied his Lord, he humbly accepted both Jesus's forgiveness and the invitation to feed Jesus's sheep. As a result, he took on a renewed boldness and passion that resulted in the salvation of thousands and, just as Jesus had predicted, the establishment of the church. He also was instrumental in opening the way for Gentiles to become believers and members of the church.

Jesus chose Peter, a young fisherman who proved to be a hothead at times and a coward at others. His story is our story. When we put our hands in the hands of Jesus, there is no telling what may happen next!

Main Takeaway

Our lives continue to change as we draw closer to Jesus, growing up into Him.

Memory Verse

So all of us who have had that veil removed can see and reflect the glory of the Lord. And the Lord—who is the Spirit—makes us more and more like him as we are changed into his glorious image.

(2 Corinthians 3:18 NLT)

Session Outline

Welcome and Opening Prayer (5-10 minutes, depending on session length)

In order to create a warm, welcoming environment as the women are gathering before the session begins, consider either lighting one or more candles, providing coffee or other refreshments, or playing worship music, or all of these. (Bring a smartphone or tablet and a portable speaker if desired.) Be sure to provide nametags if the women do not know one another or you have new participants in your group. Then, when you are ready to begin, open the group in prayer.

If meeting online, welcome each participant as she joins and encourage the women to talk informally until you are ready to open the group in prayer.

Icebreaker (5 minutes)

Invite the women to share a simple description of their life "before" and "after" Jesus by completing the following prompt. For those who have not been lifelong followers of Jesus, invite them to think about the version of themselves that may have done life apart from dependence on Jesus and His power, and the version of themselves that seeks Him daily.

- Before walking with Jesus, I.../ After walking with Jesus, I...

Video (20 minutes)

Play the Week 5 video segment. Invite participants to complete the Video Viewer Guide for Week 5 in the participant workbook as they watch (pages 169-170).

Group Discussion (25-35 minutes, depending on session length)

Note: More material is provided than you will have time to include. Before the session, select what you want to cover.

<u>Video Discussion Questions</u>

- What does it mean to grow up into Christ? How does Ephesians 4:14-15 shed light on this?

- Discuss the difference between justification and sanctification and what they have to do with growing up into Christ.
- Why do you think some Christians grow older without growing up?
- Describe someone you know who has grown up into Christ.

Participant Workbook Discussion Questions

1. On Day 1 we explored Peter's encounter with Jesus on the shore of Lake Genneserat, when Peter loaned his fishing boat to the Teacher and wound up bringing in a miraculous catch of fish. When Peter met Jesus that day and left everything to follow him, it changed his life forever. When we give our hearts to Jesus like Peter did, it changes the trajectory of our lives too.
    - Review Luke 5:1-11. What do you imagine Peter might have been feeling and thinking after a long night of fishing when Jesus asked to "borrow" his boat? When Jesus made a second request after he finished speaking to the crowd, can you hear the hint of reluctance in Peter's words in verse 5? What do you think prompted his obedience despite whatever reluctance he might have felt?
    - In what area(s) of your life do you sometimes think you know best and struggle to be obedient? When have you been unexpectedly blessed by making yourself available to God despite any hesitation you might have felt? (page 142)
    - How did you come to know Jesus personally? (page 143)
    - How has following Jesus changed you recently? (page 144)

2. We saw on Day 2 that after stepping onto the water, Peter took his eyes off Jesus and began to sink. Yet Peter had the faith to get out of the boat! He stepped out of a place of safety and comfort and then, when he faltered, he looked to Jesus to catch him. Stepping out of the boat makes all the difference. We will never walk on water if we don't get out of the boat.
    - Review Matthew 14:22-29. What do you think the other disciples were thinking when Peter stepped over the side of the boat and walked on water? What do you think Peter was thinking, for that matter? (page 147)

- According to Matthew 14:30-33, what caused Peter to falter? What do you hear in Jesus's response—criticism and disapproval, or gentle correction? Explain your answer.
- When have you taken a step in faith even though you were scared? What happened? (page 148)
- What is one area of comfort God is calling you to step away from? What fears are keeping you in your boat? (page 150)

3. Offering and receiving forgiveness is a key part of Peter's journey with Christ, as we saw on Day 3. Peter boldly asked Jesus how often he should forgive someone who sins against him, not knowing that soon he would be the one in need of mercy and forgiveness. After Jesus was arrested and put on trial, Peter denied even knowing who Jesus was. Yet Jesus forgave Peter and restored him into a right relationship with Himself. God is always ready to forgive us, and God expects us to forgive those who hurt us.
   - Read aloud Matthew 6:14-15. What is the promise and the warning in these verses? (page 154)
   - Review Matthew 18:21-22. What stands out to you in this scene, and why? What must it have felt like to Jesus for Peter to deny even knowing who Jesus was?
   - Turn to John 21 and discuss the following (pages 156–157):
     ◊ Who was the first to make his way to Jesus on the shore? (v. 7) What might this reveal to us about Peter?
     ◊ What was Jesus doing, and how did he receive the disciples? (vv. 13-15)
     ◊ What did Jesus ask Peter, and how did Peter respond? (vv. 15-17) Why do you think it is significant that Jesus asked this question three times?
   - Recall a time when you experienced a deep hurt, even a betrayal. What emotions did you experience through this situation? How did you respond? Do you have any regrets about how you handled the situation? (pages 153-154)

4. On Day 4 we saw that when Jesus asked his disciples two all-important questions, it was Simon Peter who spoke up and declared that Jesus was the

Messiah, the Son of the Living God. Then Jesus made a declaration about Peter that would come to prove that Jesus can redeem and use anyone. The key to being used isn't having it all together; it's knowing Jesus personally and making yourself available.

- Read Matthew 16:13-16. What did Jesus ask first, and how did the disciples respond? What was Jesus's second and more personal question? Who answered, and what did he say? (page 159)
- Now read aloud Jesus's response in Matthew 16:18-20. What did Jesus call Peter and what did Jesus say he would build through Peter? What did Jesus promise would *not* happen? What did Jesus promise to give Peter, and what would Peter do as a result? (Refer to your marks on page 160.)
- What hope does Jesus's declaration in Matthew 16:18 give you today? What are you facing, or what is the world facing, about which you need to know Jesus can and will overcome? (page 161)
- How might you make yourself available for Jesus to use *you* in building His church? (page 161)

5. In our final lesson this week, we were witnesses to Peter's first sermon. And what a sermon it was! Peter laid out the gospel, held people accountable for their sin, and shared how to receive salvation. The result of this Holy Spirit–infused message was that throngs of people stepped forward to be baptized! We are not seeing cowardice or betrayal anymore in Peter. This is the after version, bold and filled with God's Spirit.

- Refer to Peter's sermon in Acts 2:14-36. How did Peter draw upon familiar history and Scriptures in his presentation of the gospel? In verses 22-24, what does he want to be sure the people know?
- Of what does Peter assure the people in Acts 2:36-41, and what does he instruct them to do? How many were baptized that day? (pages 164-165)
- When have you acted boldly to stand for Christ and His teachings? What happened? When have you shied away from what you felt God was calling you to do? What happened? (page 165)
- Turn to Acts 10. When do we see Peter hesitate in this story? What does God convince Peter of, and how? (page 166)

- How might God use what you have learned through your messes to minister to others?

Deeper Conversation (15 minutes)

Divide into smaller groups of 2 to 3 for deeper conversation about practical application using some "So, what...?" questions. (Encourage the women to break into different groups each week.) If you'd like, before the session, write the questions on a markerboard or chart paper.

- So, *what* did you learn/discover this week—about God, yourself, or others?
- So, *what* is God inviting or calling you to do in response?
- So, *what* encouragement have you received for moving forward?

Closing Prayer (5 minutes)

Close the session by taking personal prayer requests from group members and leading the group in prayer. Encourage members to participate by praying out loud for one another and the requests given.

WEEK 6

Paul

Giving Christ Our All

Acts 7; 9
Various Epistles
of Paul

Leader Prep (Before the Session)

Overview

This week we met Paul, also known as Saul—a well-educated Pharisee and zealous persecutor of Christians who had a dramatic encounter with Jesus on the road to Damascus that forever changed the direction of his life. As passionately as he had persecuted believers, Saul set out with the same zeal to make more of them. This was a radical change that proved to be both life and relationship altering for him. Saul, whom the Christians once had feared, became the greatest missionary the church has ever seen. He not only established numerous churches and discipled countless leaders but he also wrote some of the most insightful and powerful letters ever written, giving the early church—and us today—the tools with which to build our faith and character.

As we focused on the life of Paul, we saw that he did not go it alone but demonstrated that Christianity is a team endeavor requiring mutual support. He even had a myriad of women as his co-laborers in Christ. Paul also demonstrated perseverance and contentment despite many obstacles and trials. He learned to live with an eternal perspective, focusing not on his hardships but on the bigger picture of what God had called him to do and what God had promised for his future.

Paul's life change and unwavering commitment to Christ were visible indicators of what God had done in his heart. He was radically changed, and this transformation led to a prolific ministry. What happened for Paul is meant to happen for *all* of us!

Main Takeaway

God wants to transform us and turn our messes into ministry as we give our all to Christ.

Memory Verse

Therefore, if anyone is in Christ, the new creation has come: The old has gone, the new is here!

(2 Corinthians 5:17)

What You Will Need

- *More Messy People* DVD and DVD player, or equipment to stream the video online
- Bible and *More Messy People* participant workbook for reference
- Markerboard or chart paper and markers (optional)
- Stick-on nametags and markers (optional)
- Smartphone or tablet and portable speaker (optional)

Session Outline

Welcome and Opening Prayer (5-10 minutes, depending on session length)

In order to create a warm, welcoming environment as the women are gathering before the session begins, consider either lighting one or more candles, providing coffee or other refreshments, or playing worship music, or all of these. (Bring a smartphone or tablet and a portable speaker if desired.) Be sure to provide nametags if the women do not know one another or you have new participants in your group. Then, when you are ready to begin, open the group in prayer.

If meeting online, welcome each participant as she joins and encourage the women to talk informally until you are ready to open the group in prayer.

Icebreaker (5 minutes)

Invite the women to share short responses to the following question:

- What are you known for? What would others say you are passionate about?

Video (20 minutes)

Play the Week 6 video segment. Invite participants to complete the Video Viewer Guide for Week 6 in the participant workbook as they watch (pages 202-203).

Group Discussion (25-35 minutes, depending on session length)

Note: More material is provided than you will have time to include. Before the session, select what you want to cover.

- Have you ever been passionate about something only to discover later that you were passionately wrong?
- When you haven't been on the right track, how has God gotten your attention?
- What are the three ways we can be proactive in seeking God and living in righteousness? Share what each of these looks like in your life.

Participant Workbook Discussion Questions

1. On Day 1 we were introduced to Saul, a Pharisee and leader in the community known for being zealous about his Jewish faith and persecuting followers of the Way (Christians). After his dramatic Damascus Road experience, when he encountered Jesus in a blinding light, he was transformed from persecutor of Christians to evangelist extraordinaire. Paul had the humility to admit he was wrong and accept God's truth and grace over his own understanding.

   - What do we learn about Stephen in Acts 6 and 7? Why did opposition rise against him? Why did they stone Stephen? (page 175) What does Acts 7:58 reveal to us about Saul?
   - What happened to Paul on the road to Damascus? (Share from your notes on page 176.)
   - Would others say you are easily correctable? If not, why do you think that is? (page 174)
   - Is there an area of your life in which you have been wrong? How might God be inviting you to move in the right direction with Christ's help? (page 177)

2. In our lesson on Day 2 we considered a number of Paul's coworkers in ministry and the significant role they played. Christianity is meant to be lived out as a team—or as Paul says in Ephesians, as a family. One of the precious gifts God gives us when we accept Jesus as Savior is a spiritual family. Paul knew this, and his ministry was exponentially enhanced because he did not go it alone.

- Who has encouraged you and partnered with you in your spiritual journey? (page 179)
- What did you learn about the ministry partners of Paul? (Refer to your notes on page 180.)
- According to Ephesians 1:5, what has always been God's plan? And how does God feel about this? (Refer to page 181.)
- What are some of the "one another" commands that show us how much God cares about us caring for one another as sisters and brothers in Christ? (page 182)
- How does being part of a local church help us live out our faith as believers? (page 182) What next step do you feel called to take to increase your devotion to God's family? (page 184)

3. On Day 3 we explored the sensitive and complex issue of women in ministry, considering how Paul viewed women by examining Scripture through Scripture. Though Paul appears to restrict the role of women, as seen in passages such as 1 Corinthians 14 and 1 Timothy 2, other Scriptures inform us just how vital women have been in ministry, especially in the first century. Paul had a myriad of women as co-laborers in ministry, giving honorable mention to many of them. The bottom line is that God loves and uses both men and women to serve His purposes as He chooses.
   - Read aloud 1 Corinthians 14:34-35 and 1 Timothy 2:11-14. If all you had to go on were these verses, what would you say was Paul's view of women? (page 186)
   - What questions have you had about the role of women in ministry? How have women in ministry been a blessing in your life? (page 187)
   - What women are mentioned in Luke 2:36 and Acts 21:8-9, and what do we learn about them? (page 187)
   - How many women did Paul commend in Romans 16? What other notable women are recorded in Scripture? (page 188)
   - Read aloud Galatians 3:26-29. What do these verses, also written by Paul, reassure us? (page 188)

4. On Day 4 we bore witness to the severe hardships Paul faced throughout his ministry. Yet despite these challenges, he learned to live with an eternal

perspective that focused on the bigger picture of what God had called him to do and what God had promised for his future. He faced obstacles with joy, demonstrating how faith in the difficulties of life develops perseverance; and perseverance is how we become more like Christ.

- What has been one of the toughest seasons of your life? How did it affect your relationship with God? (page 191)
- How would you respond if someone asked you why bad things happen to God's people? (page 192)
- According to John 16:33, what can we expect in this world, and why can we take heart? (page 192)
- Turn to 2 Corinthians 11:23b-28. What hardships did Paul experience in life? (page 193) What can we learn from Paul about persevering in faith through trials? How would you summarize Paul's eternal, joyful perspective in light of Philippians 1:12-30? (page 195)
- Read Romans 8:35, 37. What promises can we claim here? How does this influence our choice to have joy in all circumstances? (pages 193-194
- According to James 1:2-4, how can we consider it joy when we face trials? (page 195)

5. On our final day of study we considered the overall impact of Paul's life, noting that a huge part of his ministry was his testimony. His life was a visible indicator of what God had done in his heart, and others not only noticed his transformation but also were changed themselves by it. No matter the messes in our lives, God stands ready with open arms to welcome us, call us His own, and turn our mess into a masterpiece that blesses others.

- What are some of the "Come and see" moments of change you listed on page 198? Have you seen any evidence that these changes in you have touched others in some way? Take turns sharing with one another.
- What are some of your favorite passages from Paul's writings? (page 200)
- According to Romans 8:29, what is our destiny as Christ followers? How has studying the lives of messy people in the Bible encouraged you to believe that God can accomplish this purpose in you? How do you sense God working to turn your messes into ministries and masterpieces?

- Read aloud Luke 10:27. How is God inviting you to deepen your love and devotion to Him?

Deeper Conversation (15 minutes)

Divide into smaller groups of 2 to 3 for deeper conversation about practical application using some "So, what…?" questions. (Encourage the women to break into different groups each week.) If you'd like, before the session, write the questions on a markerboard or chart paper.

- So, *what* did you learn/discover this week—about God, yourself, or others?
- So, *what* is God inviting or calling you to do in response?
- So, *what* encouragement have you received for moving forward?

Closing Prayer (5 minutes)

Close the session by taking personal prayer requests from group members and leading the group in prayer. Encourage members to participate by praying out loud for one another and the requests given.

Video Viewer Guide: Answers

Week 1

grateful

rejoice

Week 2

good enough

more, enough

answers

completely, immediately

criticized

critics, great things

qualified

limitations

don't want

Week 3

courage, confront

provide

recharge

powerful

legacy, faith

Week 4

priorities

desire

time, place

phone

notepad

no

people

Week 5

immediately, faithfully

growing up

every way, Christ

never sinned

growing, Jesus

Week 6

attention

Seek, first

assessment

accountable

More from Jennifer Cowart

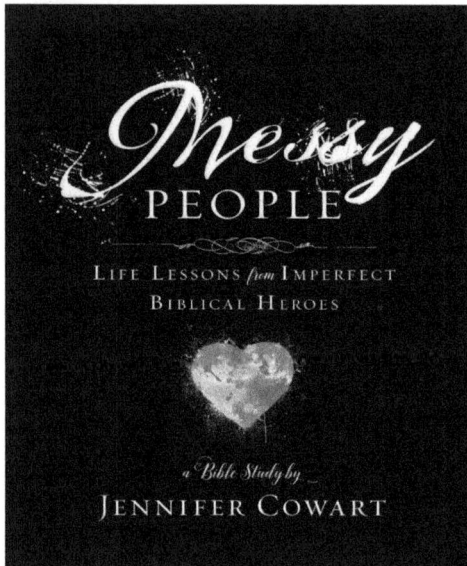

Every life gets messy at times. Sometimes these messes are literal, like a house that would be easier to condemn than to clean. But sometimes they are intangible messes such as illness, conflict, depression, abuse, bankruptcy, divorce, and job loss. In this six-week study, we will dig into the lives of biblical heroes who were messy people just like us but who were used by God in powerful ways. Along the way we'll discover that with God's guidance and help, our messes can become His masterpieces!

Participant Workbook 9781501863127
Leader Guide 9781501863141
DVD 9781501863165

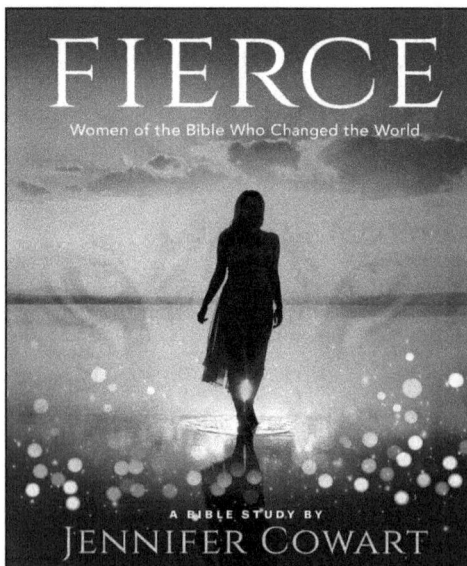

The word *fierce* is trendy. It is used to describe women who are extreme athletes, high-level executives, or supermodels. Women at the top of their game. But what about the rest of us? Can we be fierce? Absolutely! In fact, women like us have been changing the world for thousands of years—many who received little fanfare yet lived fiercely anyway. In this six-week study we will look at lesser-known female characters in the Bible and the ways they changed the world by living into God's calling, and we will discover how we, too, can live into our callings, honor the Lord, and even change the world through our courage, faithfulness, and obedience.

Participant Workbook 9781501882906
Leader Guide 9781501882920
DVD 9781501882944

More from Jennifer Cowart

We all want to be loved. We long to be desired, pursued—whether by a special someone, our friends, or others in our lives. This longing for love and acceptance is the underlying story of many of our lives, and it's the overarching story we see throughout the Scriptures. Although the Bible tells many stories, the main theme is God's relentless love for us. In this six-week study, we will explore God's great love for us from Genesis to Revelation. We will see that God passionately pursues people who do not deserve His love, and we are those people!

Participant Workbook 9781791014759
Leader Guide 9781791014773
DVD 9781791014797

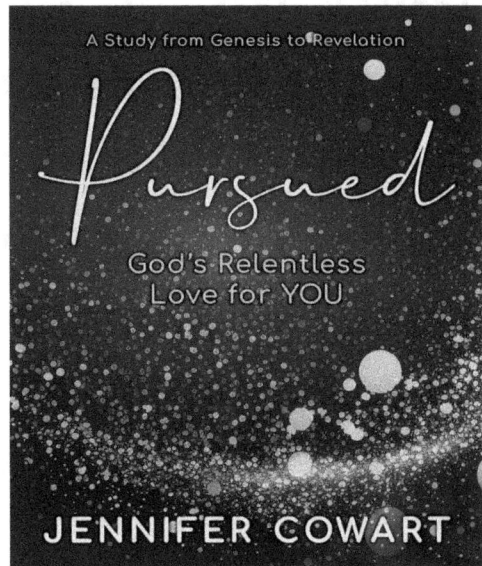

Author and teacher Jen Cowart helps women develop the habits and attitudes necessary to thrive, whatever their circumstances. Leading readers through the Book of James, a letter written about enduring hardships, she lifts up six characteristics of mature Christians: endurance, wisdom, action, control, humility, and prayer. Through this six-week study, women will find the divine and the practical in living faithfully:

Participant Workbook 9781791027803
Leader Guide 9781791027797
DVD 9781791027766

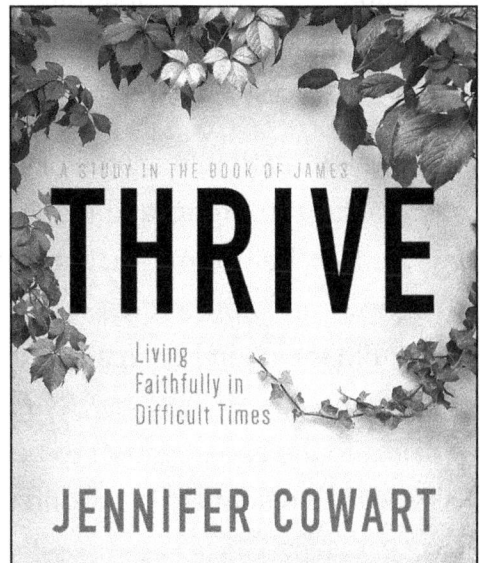

Looking for Streaming Video of Abingdon Women's Studies?
Check out **AmplifyMedia.com** to find more great videos.

Watch videos based on
More Messy People:
Life Lessons from Imperfect Biblical Heroes with Jennifer Cowart through Amplify Media.

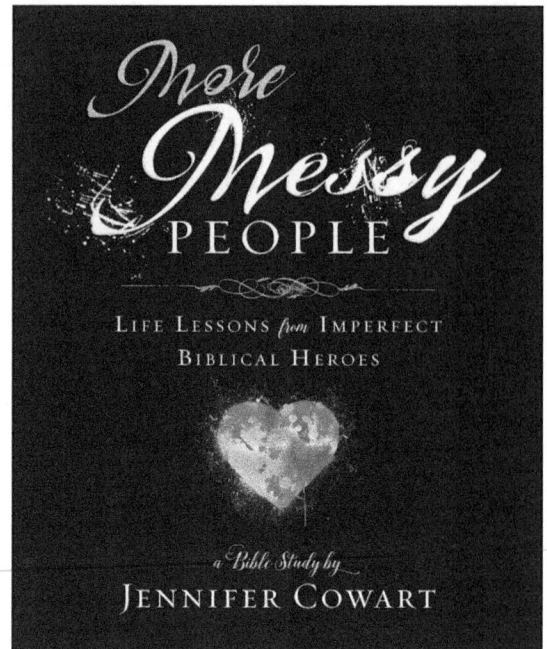

Amplify Media is a multimedia platform that delivers high-quality, searchable content with an emphasis on Wesleyan perspectives for churchwide, group, or individual use on any device at any time. In a world of sometimes overwhelming choices, Amplify gives church leaders and congregants media capabilities that are contemporary, relevant, effective, and, most important, affordable and sustainable.

With *Amplify Media* church leaders can:

- Provide a reliable source of Christian content through a Wesleyan lens for teaching, training, and inspiration in a customizable library
- Deliver their own preaching and worship content in a way the congregation knows and appreciates
- Build the church's capacity to innovate with engaging content and accessible technology
- Equip the congregation to better understand the Bible and its application
- Deepen discipleship beyond the church walls

⋀ AMPLIFY™ MEDIⲀ

**Ask your group leader or pastor about Amplify Media
and sign up today at www.AmplifyMedia.com.**

www.ingramcontent.com/pod-product-compliance
Lightning Source LLC
Chambersburg PA
CBHW081137090426
42737CB00018B/3357